LAGRANGE PARK PUBLIC LIBRARY DISTRICT

3 6086 00151 1184

W9-ATD-921

WITHDRAWN

JB
POL

Zannos, Susan

The life and times of
Marco Polo

LA GRANGE PARK PUBLIC
LIBRARY DISTRICT
555 N. LA GRANGE RD.
LA GRANGE PARK, IL 60526

DEMCO

BIOGRAPHY FROM ANCIENT CIVILIZATIONS

LEGENDS, FOLKLORE, AND STORIES OF ANCIENT WORLDS

The Life and Times of

MARCO POLO

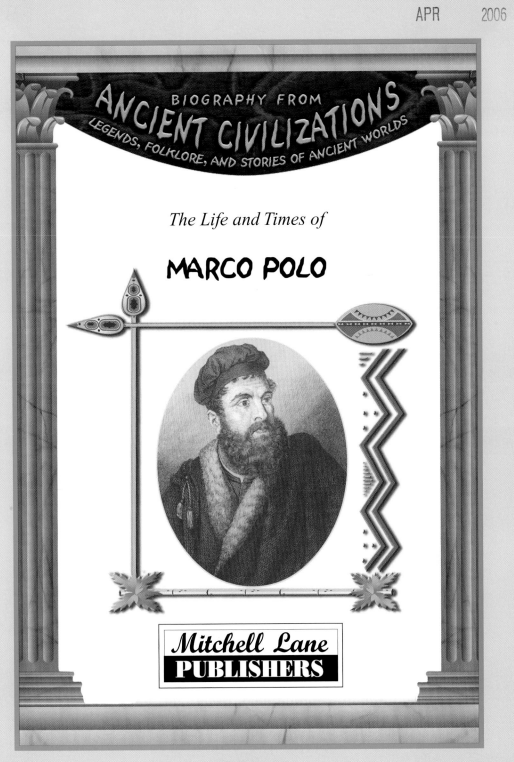

Mitchell Lane
PUBLISHERS

P.O. Box 196
Hockessin, Delaware 19707

LAGRANGE PARK PUBLIC LIBRARY
555 N. LAGRANGE ROAD
LAGRANGE PARK, IL 60526
(708) 352-0100

Titles
in the Series

The Life and Times of:

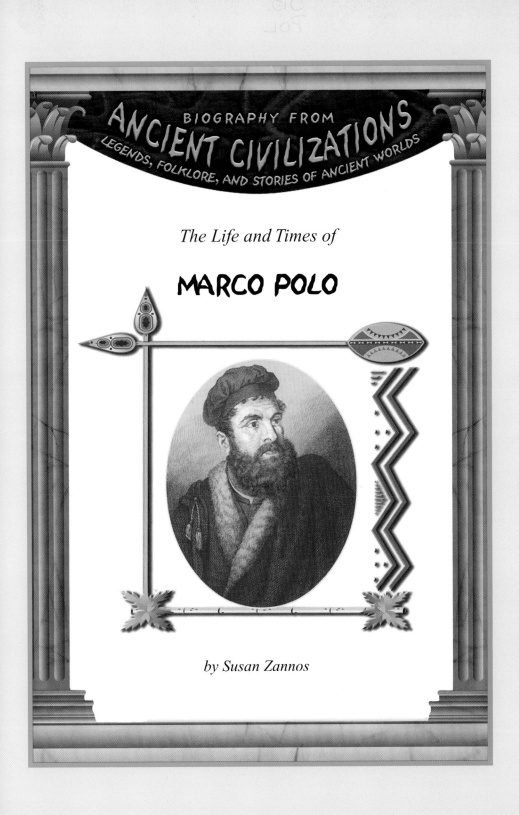

BIOGRAPHY FROM

ANCIENT CIVILIZATIONS

LEGENDS, FOLKLORE, AND STORIES OF ANCIENT WORLDS

The Life and Times of

MARCO POLO

by Susan Zannos

Mitchell Lane
PUBLISHERS

Copyright © 2005 by Mitchell Lane Publishers, Inc. All rights reserved. No part of this book may be reproduced without written permission from the publisher. Printed and bound in the United States of America.

Printing 1   2   3   4   5   6   7   8

Library of Congress Cataloging-in-Publication Data

Zannos, Susan.
      The life and times of Marco Polo / Susan Zannos.
          p. cm. — (Biography from ancient civilizations)
      Includes bibliographical references and index.
      Contents: The return—The adventure begins—Kublai Khan—The journeys—Prison.
      ISBN 1-58145-264-8 (lib. bdg.)
      1. Polo, Marco, 1254–1323?—Juvenile literature. 2. Explorers—Italy—Biography—Juvenile literature. 3. Travel, Medieval—Juvenile literature. [1. Polo, Marco, 1254–1323?—2. Explorers. 3. Voyages and travels. 4. Civilization, Medieval. 5. China—Civilization—960–1644.] I. Title. II. Series.
G370.P9Z25 2004
910.4—dc21   2003024130

ABOUT THE AUTHOR: Susan Zannos has been a lifelong educator, having taught at all levels, from preschool to college, in Mexico, Greece, Italy, Russia, and Lithuania, as well as in the United States. She has published a mystery *Trust the Liar* (Walker and Co.) and *Human Types: Essence and the Enneagram* (Samuel Weiser). Her book, *Human Types*, was recently translated into Russian, and in 2003 Susan was invited to tour Russia and lecture about her book. Another book she wrote for young adults, *Careers in Education* (Mitchell Lane) was selected for the New York Public Library's "Books for the Teen Age 2003 List." She has written many books for children, including *Chester Carlson and the Development of Xerography* and *The Life and Times of Ludwig van Beethoven* (Mitchell Lane). When not traveling, Susan lives in the Sierra Foothills of Northern California.

PHOTO CREDITS: Cover, pp. 1, 3—Art Resource; pp. 6, 9, 10, 14, 20, 21, 25, 26, 28, 33, 37, 41—Corbis; p. 11—ChinaPage.com; p. 12—Stock Montage Inc.; p. 24—Met Museum; p. 36—Superstock.

PUBLISHER'S NOTE: This story is based on the author's extensive research, which she believes to be accurate. Documentation of such research is contained on page 47.

The internet sites referenced herein were active as of the publication date. Due to the fleeting nature of some web sites, we cannot guarantee they will all be active when you are reading this book.

BIOGRAPHY FROM
ANCIENT CIVILIZATIONS
LEGENDS, FOLKLORE, AND STORIES OF ANCIENT WORLDS

The Life and Times of

MARCO POLO

*For Your Information

The magnificent medieval city of Constantinople (now called Istanbul) was located on the richest trade route between Europe and Asia, where the Mediterranean Sea and the Black Sea are connected by a narrow body of water called the Bosporus. Wealthy traders, like the Polo family of Venice, made their fortunes there.

CHAPTER
ONE

THE RETURN

Marco woke early with a strange feeling of excitement. His grandmother and the rest of the family weren't awake yet. He knew the cook didn't like to fix everyone's breakfast separately, so he grabbed an apple on his way through the kitchen. Munching on the apple, he headed along the canal toward the harbor to see what ships had arrived.

Someday, he thought as he surveyed the ships at anchor in the expansive harbor of Venice, he'd be on one of them. He'd be sailing for Constantinople with a rich cargo of trade goods. And he'd come back with the ship full of silk and spices, precious jewels and gold. He was 15, nearly old enough to make the trip. His uncle Marco, after whom he was named, said he had to wait. This morning, with the sun glinting on the little waves that lapped against the ships and a fresh breeze blowing, he felt like he couldn't wait.

He walked past a group of sailors who were loading their gear into a skiff that would take them out to their ship.

"Did you hear?" one of them was saying, "The Polos are back. Niccolò and Maffeo got in at dawn."

"I never thought we'd see them again," another said. "Thought they were dead years ago. How long has it been? Twelve years?"

"More like 15, I'd say, but they're back. I saw them just a while ago." The sailor noticed Marco. "Say, aren't you Niccolò's boy?"

But Marco was already running.

He had dreamed of this day. His father—the father he had never seen, who had left Venice before he was born—had come home! Marco burst into the house and stopped as though suddenly turned to stone. The entrance hall was stacked full of crates, trunks, and boxes. In the dining room, two strange men were sitting at the table. The cook bustled about serving them.

One of the men stood and held his arms wide. "Marco? I am your father."

Marco could barely speak. "How do you do, sir?" he whispered. Unable to think of anything else to do, he bowed.

Niccolò Polo laughed. "Come here, then. You have fine manners, but give your father a hug."

In the days and weeks that followed, Marco was like his father's shadow. They went everywhere together. As they walked the streets of Venice, his father told him all that had happened since he and his brother Maffeo had left the city in the autumn of 1253.

Marco's grandfather, Andrea Polo, had established a family trading business in Constantinople and in Soldaia on the Crimean Peninsula in the Black Sea. Niccolò and Maffeo set off for Constantinople with a cargo of merchandise. Young Niccolò had recently married, and the young wife he left behind was pregnant. Maffeo was even younger, hardly more than a boy.

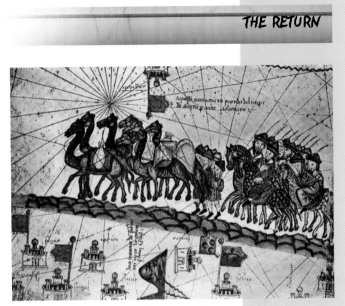

This painting is a detail from an illustrated map showing the 13th-century caravan of Niccolò and Maffeo Polo crossing Asia. During their 15 year journey, Niccolò's son, Marco Polo, was growing up in Venice.

Niccolò and Maffeo Polo made many short trading trips in the area of the eastern Mediterranean. They ventured into ports in the Black Sea. They were disappointed in the business opportunities. Too many other traders had been there before them. If they were going to make their fortune, they would have to push on further eastward, into the lands controlled by the Mongols. They traveled by horseback from the eastern shore of the Black Sea to the Volga River, which is located in the modern-day Ukraine.

The ruler of this westernmost part of the Mongol Empire was Berke Khan. He was a grandson of the great Genghis Khan, whose armies had conquered millions of square miles of territory. Like other Mongol rulers, Berke was curious about foreigners. He welcomed the Polo brothers, who gave him precious jewels they had brought from Constantinople. Berke in turn gave them many rich gifts. He also allowed them to go on trading expeditions in his land.

The exotic city of Bukhara (located in modern Uzbekistan) provided a safe haven for Niccolò and Maffeo Polo for three years while warring Mongol rules fought on all sides and they could not continue their journey.

With Berke Khan's assistance, the Polos made a good profit. They decided to return to Venice. Unfortunately the way home was no longer safe. A war had started between Berke and a cousin who controlled the land to the south. The country between the Volga and the Black Sea was the scene of fierce Mongol battles. The Polos couldn't go back the way they had come.

Niccolò and Maffeo left Berke's territory and traveled south and east until they reached the city of Bukhara—located a little to the north of modern-day Afghanistan—two months later. Having gotten that far, they were in a fine fix. Wars between rival Mongol rulers raged on all sides. Another khan, Borrakh, controlled Bukhara. The Polo brothers were safe in Bukhara because they were under the khan's protection. They stayed for three years until the wars were finally over.

Some time late in 1264, an official from the court of the greatest khan of all, Kublai Khan, arrived in Bukhara. This ambassador knew nothing of the people of Europe. He was fascinated by the Polos, the first Europeans he had ever seen. He soon made them an offer: He would conduct them to see Kublai

Khan, who also had never seen any Europeans. He would also guarantee their complete safety during the trip. So off they went.

The journey from Bukhara to Kublai Khan's palace in Beijing took a year. Kublai Khan received them kindly. By this time Niccolò and Maffeo spoke Mongolian fluently, so they were able to talk about their native country with him. Kublai Khan was very interested in hearing about the kings and princes of the west. He wanted to know how they governed their people, and how they fought their battles. He was particularly interested in hearing about the Christian religion and the Pope.

The great Mongol leader Kublai Kahn, shown in this Chinese painting, was the most powerful ruler after his grandfather, Ghengis Kahn. He adopted many of the civilized practices of the great Chinese dynasty that he conquered.

After many conversations with the Polos, Kublai Khan decided to send them on a mission. He asked them to take letters from him to the Pope. He wanted the Pope to send a hundred men of learning who could teach his people about western knowledge and the Christian religion. He also asked the Polo brothers to bring him some holy oil from the lamp over the burial place of Jesus in Jerusalem. They gladly agreed to do as Kublai Khan requested.

On their trip back, they carried a golden tablet from the Great Khan. It guaranteed them safe passage. It also guaranteed them the best lodgings and horses and escorts to guide them. Even so, their journey home was long and difficult. It took them three years to reach Acre, a port at the eastern end of the Mediterranean. There they learned that the pope, Clement VI, had recently died. They conferred with Teobaldo, the pope's representative in Acre, about their mission. As Marco would later write, "He was filled with wonder, and it seemed to him that this affair was greatly to the profit and honor of Christendom. He said to them: 'Sirs, you see that the Pope is dead. Therefore your only wise course is to wait in patience until such time as there is a Pope.' "[1]

Since they had to wait, they thought they might as well return to Venice to see their families. Niccolò was saddened to learn that his wife had died, but he was delighted to meet the eager teenager who was his son. The boy reminded Niccolò of himself when he had been the same age. Marco listened carefully to all that his father told him about his travels. He asked intelligent questions, and begged his father to start teaching him the Mongol language. Before long Niccolò decided to take the boy when he and Maffeo returned to the court of Kublai Khan.

This historical artwork shows the Polo brothers leaving Constantinople with young Marco Polo in 1271. Their journey from there to the court of Kublai Kahn in China would take them three and a half years. It would be 20 more years until the Polos would see Constantinople again on their return journey in 1295.

The Crusades

Some of the strangest events of the Middle Ages were the religious wars known as the Crusades. Armies from Europe traveled to the lands at the eastern end of the Mediterranean Sea. Their stated purpose was to save the city of Jerusalem from the infidels. In Latin, the word "infidel" meant "without faith." The crusaders thought anyone who was not a Christian was an infidel.

Pope Urban II

The Popes, the leaders of the Christian Church, were afraid of the power the Islamic religion was gaining in Asia and North Africa. In 1095, Pope Urban II urged a crusade to free the holy city of Jerusalem from the Islamic "infidels," who had recently captured it. He appealed to the religious faith of the people as well as to their greed. Crusaders would save their souls by fighting for Christ, and they would also bring home gold and other treasures. The combination of salvation and wealth attracted peasants, too. During the First Crusade in 1096, a group of poor peasants left Europe before the army of noblemen.

One reason that young noblemen were so eager to set out for adventure and riches was the custom that only the oldest son could inherit land and other property. The younger sons of European nobility had no hope of sharing in the family fortune. The Crusades offered them an opportunity to gain their own wealth.

The First Crusade was the only successful one. The Crusaders captured Jerusalem and three other major cities: Edessa, Tripoli, and Antioch. In 1144, an Islamic army recaptured Edessa. Two years later, French and German nobles led armies to recapture Edessa. This crusade was a disaster, as were all the ones that followed. Islamic armies under the command of Saladin recaptured Jerusalem in 1187.

Some of the oddities and horrors that took place over the next 200 years included the Fourth Crusade of 1202, in which the crusaders ended up attacking the Christian city of Constantinople for plunder instead of going to Jerusalem. In 1212, the tragic Children's Crusade gathered thousands of children and teenagers, nearly all of whom starved or drowned.

St. Mark's Cathedral in Venice is one of the architectural wonders of the world. Completed about 1090 A.D., it is lavishly decorated with mosaics depicting stories from the Bible. The square in front of the cathedral is the true center of the city, where people gathered and important public events took place.

CHAPTER
TWO

THE ADVENTURE BEGINS

Marco Polo was born in Venice in 1254, the year following his father's departure. Marco grew up without a father, and his mother died when he was young. But the Polo family was wealthy, with plenty of servants to care for the boy. In 1260, when Marco was six or seven years old, news reached Venice that his father and uncle had left Constantinople. From that time nothing further was heard. People told Marco that his father was surely dead. But in his heart he didn't believe it.

Marco did not write about his boyhood years, but scholars have done careful research about life in 13th century Venice, so we have a good idea of the conditions under which he was raised. For one thing, he probably had very little formal schooling.

As author John Larner points out, "In Venice merchants' sons, destined to follow in their fathers' footsteps, normally had the most superficial contact with the Latin learning of the grammar schools. Their education was almost wholly devoted to their future vocation."[1]

As a result, notes writer Henry Hart, "He [Marco] acquired his education on the canals and the quays, the bridges and the open squares of the city."[2] He could read and write, because he would later take extensive notes wherever he went. He probably knew some French as well, and eventually he would learn four Asian languages.

There was much to learn in Venice. The great St. Mark's Cathedral was an education in itself. "In every corner and on every available bit of wall or arch was a Bible story. Even the most ignorant could learn their religious history as in a great picture book, its leaves those magnificent mosaics which still look down upon us seven centuries after the master workmen set them in their place, bit by bit, in fadeless colors and in brightest gold."[3] Marco certainly became a devoted Christian as a result of his early years.

The piazza, or open space, in front of St. Mark's provided another kind of education. Gambling tables, where fortunes were won and lost, were set up between two great columns. Public executions and other punishments also took place in the Piazza. Venice, a city of sailors and traders, had its share of sinful activities. Marco did not grow up ignorant of the ways of the world.

Another favorite place for boys in Venice was the Rialto, the business district. "In the Rialto thronged merchants and visitors from every corner of the world—from the Levant and Greece, from Spain and France, and from cold northern Germany and England. Business was on everyone's lips. Venice seemed to live only on business and for business, and the boy Marco grew up in its atmosphere. To be a great merchant was every Venetian's ambition, and Marco dreamed of the day when he, too, like the father and the uncle whom he had never seen, would fare out into the unknown world of the East and become a merchant prince."[4]

When his father and uncle finally returned, Marco still had to wait two more years before setting out on his great adventure. As the time went by and no new Pope was elected, the Polo brothers decided to wait no longer. "When they had waited all this time and saw that no Pope was being made, they decided that if they waited longer it might be too late for them to return to the Great Khan. So they set out from Venice, taking with them Marco the son of Niccolò,"[5] Marco wrote much later in *The Travels of Marco Polo*, the book that made him famous. Curiously, he always referred to himself in the third person, as if he was a character in the book rather than its narrator.

In Acre, the Polos consulted with Teobaldo, who agreed with their decision to proceed. He provided them with the oil from the tomb of Jesus the Great Khan requested. Shortly after the Polos had set out on the long journey, Teobaldo received news from Italy: He was the new Pope. He took the name Gregory X. He called the Polos back so he could officially answer the letters that Kublai Khan had sent. The new Pope didn't have a hundred learned men to send. He only had two friars who happened to be in Acre at the time. He also sent valuable presents. And so, even though they were short 98 holy friars, the Polos set out again.

They had barely begun the journey inland from Acre when trouble started. War again. Niccolò and Maffeo had experienced enough of that sort of thing that they weren't afraid. But the two friars were terrified and refused to go further. "They were men of God, and had no personal obligations towards the Great Khan, or any prospect of making a fortune by visiting him. They made all their credentials and documents over to the Polos, took their leave of them and returned to Acre,"[6] writes R. P. Lister.

The three Polos continued on their journey. As they passed through Armenia, they saw what Marco was told was Mt. Ararat, where Noah's Ark had reputedly landed after the great flood described in the Bible. Even though the summit was so high it was covered by snow all year round, something black—supposedly the ark—could be seen near the top.

They passed near the southern end of the Caspian Sea, where Marco reported that "there is a spring of oil from which gushes a stream of oil, in such abundance that a hundred ships may load there at once. This oil is not good to eat; but it is good for burning and as a salve for men and camels affected with itch or scab. Men come from a long distance to fetch this oil, and in all the neighborhood no other oil is burned but this."[7] Today this area is the center of the Russian petroleum industry, the Baku oil fields.

They continued south to the Persian Gulf where it empties into the Arabian Sea, and arrived in the city of Hormuz in 1272. At Hormuz, they hoped to find ships in which to make the journey to China. They were disappointed. "Their ships are very bad, and many of them founder, because they are not fastened with iron nails but stitched together with thread made of coconut husks," Marco wrote. "This makes it a risky undertaking to sail in these ships. And you can take my word that many of them sink, because the Indian Ocean is often very stormy."[8] As Venetians, they knew better than to set out into a treacherous sea in flimsy boats.

They turned back to the north, forced into taking an overland route. They had to cross great deserts that stretched before them through long weary days of travel. During the winter months, they made little progress because of snow and biting cold in the mountain passes. Marco rarely commented on the difficulties and discomforts of traveling. He concentrated on reporting what he saw in the areas they passed through. Nonetheless, they did have problems. At one point, when describing the pure water and air to be found high in the mountains, Marco said that after having been sick for a year, he went up into the mountains and was cured.

Finally, nearly three and a half years after they had left Venice, the end of their trip was nearly at hand.

Venice

The city of Venice is located on the eastern coast of Italy. Starting in the late 400s, Venice was built on islands, which were connected to each other by bridges. Instead of streets there were canals; instead of carriages, the residents used boats to get around. All of the bridges, canals, and streets came together in the Rialto, the business district.

The successful men of Venice, the founders of great wealthy families, did their buying and selling in the Rialto. Silks and spices from the east were traded for woolen goods and grain from the west. Gold and silver and precious jewels from Asia, exotic hardwoods from Africa, marble and wrought iron from Europe—all were made available by the clever businessmen of Venice. Many of these wealthy Venetian traders had their own ships to bring in rich cargos, and to deliver them again to their buyers.

In 1204 the great city of Constantinople fell to the crusaders on their way to the Holy Land. This odd event, a Christian city being attacked by a Christian army, had been arranged by the Venetians. Constantinople was Venice's main competition for trade with the east. The Venetians bribed the crusaders with ships in exchange for the attack on Constantinople.

Venice spread her influence throughout the Mediterranean and Black Sea regions. But the city had a powerful rival: Genoa, a city on the west coast of Italy, also became a major center of trade. During the 13th and 14th centuries, Venice fought—and eventually won—a series of wars with Genoa for control of the shipping routes.

The city's wealthy merchants built fine palaces to live in, magnificent churches for the glory of God (many of them decorated with precious paintings and altarpieces brought home from the looting of Constantinople), and elaborate public buildings. Although its importance eventually declined, Venice remains one of the world's most beautiful cities. Many tourists visit it every year.

This miniature painting appeared in a medieval book titled Maudeville's Book of Marvels. The painting is titled "Marco Polo before Kublai Kahn," and shows Marco presenting a letter to the Great Kahn, perhaps the letter Pope Gregory X had sent with the Polos.

CHAPTER
THREE

KUBLAI KHAN

Although their travels had been long, Marco and his father and uncle had not been in danger. They carried letters from the Pope, which gained them assistance from Christians along the way. Much more important was the golden tablet that showed they were under the protection of the Great Khan. No one would dare attack a caravan that was under his protection. Furthermore, the best horses and the most comfortable resting places were provided for them. Still, they may have been a little uneasy at approaching the court after an absence of nearly a decade. If so, their minds were quickly set at rest.

"When the Great Khan knew that Messer (Mister) Niccolò and Messer Maffeo were coming, he sent his couriers fully forty days' journey to meet them, and they were well served and attended in every thing," Marco wrote. "Be assured that great indeed were the mirth and merry-making with which the Great Khan and all his court welcomed the arrival of these emissaries. And they were well served and attended in everything. They stayed at court and had a place of honor above the other barons."[1]

Pope Gregory X, formerly Teobaldo Visconti, was selected in 1271. One of his first official actions as Pope was to send letters and gifts to Kublai Kahn with the Polos.

Kublai Khan asked the Polos to tell of their travels and of their experiences with the Pope. When they gave him the holy oil and the presents Pope Gregory had sent him, he was well pleased. Then he noticed Marco. He asked who the young man was. Niccolò explained that Marco was his son—and the servant of the Great Khan. It was the beginning of a friendship and a mutual respect that would last for 17 years.

Marco must have been wide-eyed in astonishment at a civilization that in many respects was far in advance of the one in which he had been raised. The royal palace dwarfed anything in Europe.

It was contained within three sets of walls. The first wall formed a square eight miles long on each side. Within this enclosure was a space a mile wide before the next walls, which were six miles long, formed the second square. The army was quartered in the space between the walls, and many trees and plants formed a beautiful park. The second set of walls had three gates in the north wall and three in the south, with large buildings in the spaces between the gates. These buildings were used to store the equipment and weapons needed by the army.

The inner enclosure had walls one mile long. Within this square was the palace itself, which contained many magnificent decorated chambers around a grand dining hall. To the rear of the palace were buildings containing the Great Khan's treasure—gold and silver and precious jewels in unbelievable quantities. On the other side of this grand palace was another palace, the residence of Kublai's oldest son. An exquisite park with many pavilions and ponds surrounded these palaces.

Marco was impressed with the luxurious palaces of Kublai Khan. But he was even more impressed with the khan's ability to organize and rule his huge empire. A system of stations on all of the major roads leading to the provinces made it possible for messages to be sent and received rapidly, and for travelers to make their journeys in comfort.

Every 25 or 30 miles there was a large comfortable house where even royalty could stay in luxury. Scores or even hundreds of good horses were available at each station so the official ambassadors and other travelers would have fresh horses to ride for the next stage of their trip. These stations were even built in mountainous areas. Little villages grew up around them for the people who cared for the horses, cooked meals for the travelers, and provided services.

"And this is surely the highest privilege and the greatest resource ever enjoyed by any man on earth," Marco wrote. "For you may be well assured that more than 200,000 horses are stabled at these posts for the special use of these messengers. Moreover, the posts themselves number more than 10,000, all furnished on the same lavish scale. The whole organization is so stupendous and so costly that it baffles speech and writing."[2]

In modern terms, we might say that Kublai Khan's postal service had three classes: second class, first class, and top priority.

For second class, there were cottages every three miles for foot messengers in the service of the khan. These messengers wore a belt with bells that jingled as they ran. Hearing the bells, the next

This Mongol passport from the 13th Century is in the Metropolitan Museum in New York. It is similar to the passport Kublai Kahn gave to Marco Polo—except Marco's passport was made of gold.

messenger would be all ready to take the message or package and run the next three miles. It was like a very long relay race. Messages that would take a single messenger 100 days to deliver could be transmitted in just 10 days using this system. It also allowed fruit that was picked early one morning to be delivered to Kublai Khan on the following evening rather than the 10 days that it would normally require.

First class involved the use of horses. A rider would cover the 25 or so miles between stations, then dismount and pass the mail pouch to a new mounted messenger. When really urgent—top priority—messages, such as those concerning rebellions or serious disturbances, needed to be sent, special couriers using a series of the best horses could cover 250, 300, or even more miles in a day.

To keep this amazing system running, clerks noted the arrival and departure of each messenger. Officers arrived at least once a month to check that everything was operating smoothly and to punish anyone who wasn't tending to business.

Kublai Khan was a compassionate ruler who stored extra grain to give to people who had suffered hardships such as floods or droughts. He provided those who were unable to support themselves because of age or illness with food and clothing. He was

This fanciful picture of Marco Polo and Kublai Kahn was created by an artist in the middle ages who, like most people of that time, had never seen an elephant and had only the foggiest idea what one might look like.

able to do this because of the taxes he collected from those who were prosperous. The Mongols had not provided for the poor this way, but Kublai had learned this practice from the Chinese he had conquered. Instead of imposing his ways upon the people he ruled, he learned the best their civilization had to teach him.

As Marco learned more and more about Kublai Khan, he acquired a great respect and admiration for him. He described the Great Khan this way: "He is a man of good stature, neither short nor tall but of moderate height. His limbs are well fleshed out and modeled in due proportion. His complexion is fair and ruddy like a rose, the eyes black and handsome, the nose shapely and set squarely in place."[3]

The Great Khan had 22 sons with his four official wives. Seven of these sons governed the provinces in the empire.

Yet with all his power, Kublai Khan had one major source of frustration. He was a very intelligent and curious man. He wanted

25

LAGRANGE PARK PUBLIC LIBRARY
555 N. LAGRANGE ROAD
LAGRANGE PARK, IL 60526
(708) 352-0100

This engraving of a Tartar man from the early 18th Century shows that the descendents of Genghis Kahn's fierce Mongolian warriors had become far more civilized than their nomadic ancestors. They were still renowned for their skill as archers, however.

to know all about the territories that he governed. When he sent ambassadors or official messengers to these territories, they would carry out the missions that they were assigned. But that was all they would do. They did not bring back reports of what the country was like or how the people lived or what kinds of birds and animals, trees and plants were to be found.

When young Marco Polo arrived in his court, Kublai Khan soon realized he had found the man he had been hoping for. As Marco told the Great Khan about their journey from Venice, he included descriptions of the habits of the people they met, of the strange and wonderful stories they told, and of the land itself.

Soon Kublai Khan began sending Marco Polo on missions all over his vast empire. When Marco would return, he would tell the Great Khan everything he had observed. Marco was already fluent in the Mongolian language. He soon learned other languages so he could talk with the people he visited and learn about their ways.

Genghis Khan

Sometime between 1162 and 1167, a Mongol chieftain called Yesugei and his wife had a son they named Temujin. When Temujin was still a boy, his father took him traveling to find a girl who would be his bride. He became betrothed to Bortei, the daughter of a chieftain of another tribe. Shortly after this, Yesugei died, poisoned by Tartars, who were rivals of the Mongols. The boy vowed to avenge his father's death.

Young Temujin returned to his own tribe and declared himself chief. The elders refused to accept a boy that young as their leader. They abandoned him and his family members on the plains. Temujin's desire for vengeance then included the members of his own clan who had rejected him. The family struggled desperately for survival. When he discovered his brother stealing food from the group, Temujin killed him. It became known among the Mongols that he was a leader who would use harsh punishment to keep order and discipline.

In 1189, he was elected leader of his tribe. He called for all the Mongols to join together to defeat their enemies and began a series of military campaigns to achieve his goal. The last resisting clan was defeated by 1204. In 1206 the now-united Mongols declared Temujin their great khan (ruler), and gave him the name Genghis Khan.

Having united his people, whether they wanted it or not, Genghis Kahn began to conquer China. He took Beijing in 1215, though his aim to control all of China was achieved only by his grandson Kublai Khan. Then he turned his attention to the north and west. His soldiers were highly organized and fought fiercely. It seemed that nothing could withstand them. In 25 years, his armies conquered more territory than the Romans had been able to in 400 years.

Genghis Kahn and his wife Bortei had three surviving sons and many grandsons by the time he died in 1227. The huge Mongol empire was divided into three regions, each controlled by one of Genghis Khan's sons.

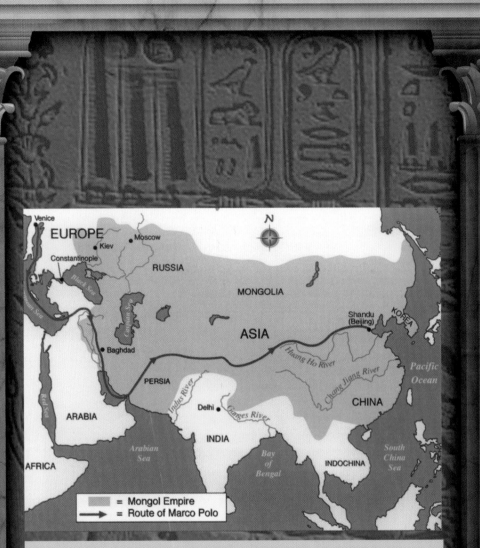

The enormous distances covered by Marco Polo and his father and uncle took them the length of the huge Mongol Empire to Kublai Khan's court in eastern China. No other Europeans had penetrated so far, and the Great Kahn's curiosity about these westerners caused him to welcome them.

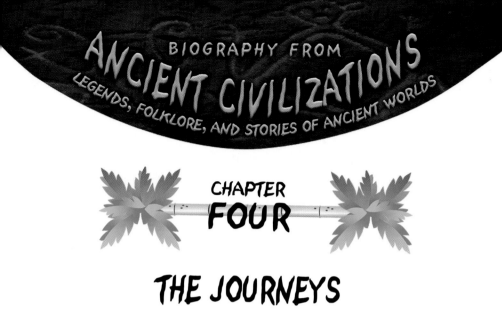

CHAPTER

FOUR

THE JOURNEYS

Marco Polo and his father and uncle served Kublai Khan faithfully and well for 17 years. During those years, Marco traveled on official business throughout the grand khan's empire. He took careful notes and brought back fascinating facts and stories about the regions that he visited. As a reward for his good service, he was appointed an official of a distant province for three years.

In his book, Marco did not give the time sequence of when he went to the many places he wrote about. In fact, he didn't even make clear which places he actually visited and which ones he had only heard about from other travelers. His main interest was in providing details about how the people lived and about the landscapes and the plants and animals.

The two main peoples Marco lived with were the Tartars, which is what he and other Europeans called the Mongols, and the Chinese, whom the Tartars had conquered. The Tartars were a nomadic people. They moved with their herds from the mountains in the summer to the warmer lowland plains in the winter. The women and children rode in two-wheeled carts that also carried their cooking pots. Their food was meat and milk.

Their dwellings were a perfect match for this on-the-go lifestyle. "They have circular houses made of wood and covered with felt, which they carry about with them on four-wheeled wagons wherever they go. For the framework of rods is so neatly and skillfully constructed that it is light to carry. And every time they unfold their house and set it up, the door is always facing south,"[1] Marco wrote.

The Tartar warriors were the most disciplined and the cruelest the world has ever seen. The men lived on and by their horses, remaining on horseback for as long as two days and nights without dismounting. The Tartars drank the milk of their mares, and, if no wild animals were found for food, opened a vein and drank their horses' blood for nourishment. Each warrior had about eighteen horses with him.

Another reason for their success was the way in which they were organized. Each ten men were obedient to one officer, who in turn took orders from another officer who commanded a hundred. This officer took his orders from yet another officer, who was responsible for a thousand. Thus, the leader of a Tartar army needed only give orders to ten men, who in turn gave the orders to the ten beneath him, and so on down to the individual warriors.

These orders were never questioned. "For they [Tartar warriors] are all obedient to the word of command more than any other people in the world,"[2] Marco observed.

This habit of obedience was matched with superior tactics. As skilled horsemen, they had a great deal of mobility. They were deadly shots with their bows and arrows. They weren't afraid to retreat during a battle, firing as they fled. When they had inflicted enough casualties on their pursuers, they would turn around and crush their enemies. "By these tactics they have already won many battles and conquered many nations,"[3] Marco noted admiringly.

These conquests had begun with Kublai Khan's grandfather Genghis Khan. Kublai Khan had increased the size of the empire and kept it at peace. One important reason that he was able to keep peace was his tolerance for different religions. Marco said that the Tartars did not care what form of worship was used or what gods were worshiped as long as men paid their tribute to the Great Khan and obeyed his laws. In this way peace prevailed among people of many different religions. Although Marco was himself a devout Christian, he admired Kublai Khan's respect for all faiths.

This tolerant attitude was in sharp contrast with that of the Christians, who disturbed the peace by insisting they had the only true religion. One friar who had caused trouble was lectured by the Great Khan: "We Mongols believe that there is only one God, by whom we live and by whom we die, and for whom we have an upright heart. . . . But as God gives us the different fingers of the hand, so he gives to men divers [different] ways. . . . God gave you the scriptures, and you do not abide by them. He gave us diviners, we do what they tell us, and we live in peace."[4]

Unlike the barbaric Tartars, the Chinese they had conquered were highly civilized and cultured people. Kublai Khan learned much from the Chinese. He learned to enjoy the beautiful palaces and parks, to eat the fruits and vegetables of their gardens, to wear luxurious robes made of silk and cloth of gold and embroidered with jewels, to issue paper money bearing his official seal, and to administer his vast kingdom efficiently in times of peace. Kublai Khan conquered the Chinese, but the Chinese civilized Kublai Khan.

Marco was astonished to find how clean the Chinese were. They took baths three or more times a week, a familiarity with water unknown to Europeans of the time. And they heated their bath water with what he called "black rocks." This was coal, which was not used at that time in Europe. He was impressed with the courtesy and refinement of their manners, the elegance of their buildings, and the cleanliness of their streets, which were paved and free of mud. He found the civilization of China far more advanced than that of his native Venice.

Nonetheless, as time passed the Polos began to think of returning to Venice. Niccolò and Maffeo were practical men. They were getting older, and Kublai Khan was by this time very old. They realized that once he died, they would be helpless. Many members of the Great Khan's court were jealous of the favor he showed the Venetians. When a powerful khan died, his relatives would often begin warring among themselves for his territories. Again and again the brothers asked Kublai Khan to let them return to their homeland. Again and again he refused. He enjoyed the company of the Europeans, and they were useful to him.

At last they saw their chance. In the year 1288, ambassadors from Persia arrived at the court of Kublai Khan. They reported that the beloved Mongol wife of the khan who ruled Persia had died. Her last wish was that her husband should take a woman from her own clan for his next wife. The ambassadors asked Kublai Khan to select a woman to send back with them. The Great Khan chose a beautiful 17-year-old princess named Kokachin. The ambassadors were well satisfied and began their return trip with the royal princess, going overland in a caravan. Eight months later they were back at Kublai Khan's court again. Warring Mongol tribes had blocked their route.

At that time, Marco had recently returned from a long sea voyage to India. The Persian ambassadors heard of his ability as a seaman and asked that they be allowed to return to Persia by sea with Marco Polo in command. Kublai Khan was in a fix. He didn't want the Polos to leave his court. On the other hand, he didn't want

This undated illustration is titled "Marco Polo 1250–1324. Italian traveler." Perhaps it represents the Polos preparing to set sail on their long voyage home in the spring of 1291. At this time Kublai Kahn sent them to take the princess Kokachin to Persia.

to anger the powerful khan of Persia. Finally he gave his consent for Niccolò, Maffeo and Marco to escort the princess to Persia, but asked them to return when they had completed their mission.

Again Kublai Khan presented the Polos with golden tablets that guaranteed their safety. He gave them fabulous jewels as gifts. Fourteen large ships were provided for their use, along with supplies to last for two years. The royal party, with Marco Polo in charge, sailed out into the South China Sea in the spring of 1291.

Their long voyage took nearly two years, during which they stopped at many islands of the South China Sea and the Indian Ocean. In his accounts of his travels Marco Polo described Java and Borneo and other islands. They sailed the strait between the Malay Peninsula and Sumatra. They rounded the southern tip of India and proceeded through the Arabian Sea to Hormuz, where nearly 20 years before they had found no suitable ships for a sea voyage.

When they reached Persia at last, they learned that the khan who had sent for the princess was dead. They traveled overland to take the princess to the khan's son, who was more her age anyway and married her. Their duty to Kublai Khan successfully completed, again the Polos were given golden tablets that gave them safe passage and assistance on their way. Then they received the news that Kublai Khan had died. They were no longer required to return to China—in fact they could not.

It was time to go home. With an escort of Mongol horsemen, "they set out on their journey and rode by daily stages till they reached Trebizond [a city on the Black Sea]. From Trebizond they sailed to Constantinople, thence to Negropont [the Greek island of Euboea], and from Negropont to Venice. This was in the year of the Incarnation of Christ 1295,"[5] Marco reported. Actually it was not all that easy. The travelers encountered serious difficulties in Trebizond, where they were robbed of a large portion of their treasure.

How strange it must have been for Marco Polo to return to Venice. Henry Hart imagines the moment: "The wearisome voyage was over, the longest journey ever made and recorded by any man in all the world's history. . . . The friends of his late youth and his mature manhood were many thousands of miles away, dwelling in strange lands, speaking strange languages, living strange lives. . . . He was cut off from them forever, return to them was impossible. . . . He had to begin life anew at forty, to settle down among a people whose ways were no longer his ways, whose thoughts were no longer his thoughts, to live in a sea-girt city of small islands after wandering widely up and down on the winds of the world for many years."[6]

SILK

The production of silk was a closely guarded secret in China for thousands of years. According to legend, about 4,700 years ago a Chinese empress watched little worms spinning their cocoons in the palace gardens. She unwound the thread of one cocoon and found it was a single, long, shiny thread. She got her ladies-in-waiting to help her. They unwound many cocoons, spun the threads together, and wove them into a beautiful piece of cloth. From the cloth they made a wonderful robe for the emperor.

Sericulture, the process of making silk from silkworm cocoons, became a carefully protected art throughout China. The precious material was in demand throughout Asia and Europe. In 139 B.C. the famous "Silk Road" opened. It stretched from about 4,000 miles from eastern China to the Mediterranean. Not only silk, but also spices, gold, jewels, and other trade goods traveled along this route.

The Chinese sold the beautiful silk but did not reveal the secret that it was made from the cocoons of little worms. Anyone telling the secret would be put to death. The Romans had some fantastic theories—silk came from flower petals that grew in the desert, it came from soft fuzz on certain leaves—but they never did learn the secret.

Gradually the secret spread. There are legends about how that happened, too. One is that the Japanese kidnapped four Chinese maidens who knew the secret and carried with them mulberry seedlings (because the silk worms eat only mulberry leaves) and silkworm eggs. Another is that a Chinese princess married an Indian prince and smuggled out silkworm eggs and mulberry shoots in her wedding headdress. In this way silk production spread to India. A third is that two traveling monks brought eggs and mulberry shoots to Constantinople in their hollow walking sticks. From Constantinople, the secret spread throughout Europe.

This beautiful fabric is still in great demand in spite of all the new manmade fibers. World silk production has doubled during the last 30 years. Japan is considered one of the world's leading producers of silk, while China, once again, is the world's main producer of silk.

The Rialto Bridge in Venice has spanned the Grand Canal since the 12th Century, although it has been rebuilt several times. It has a 24-foot arch that allows boats to pass, and the central walkway is lined with merchants' shops.

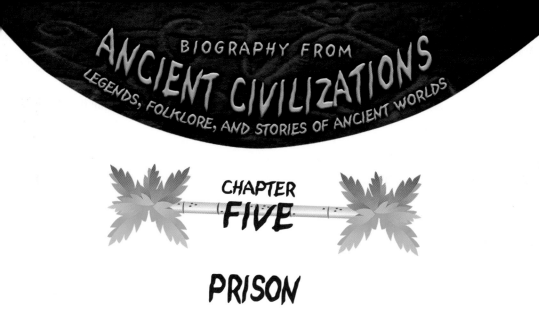
CHAPTER
FIVE

PRISON

Venice seemed strange to the returning travelers. Niccolò and Maffeo were now old men who had spent virtually all their adult lives in the Far East. They had been away for over 40 years. Marco, now in his 40s, had been gone since he was 17. They hardly remembered their native language or the customs of their own city. And of course many changes had occurred in Venice during their absence.

If Venice seemed strange to them, the returning travelers seemed even stranger to Venice. The members of their own family did not recognize them. When they came to the door of their own home, they were turned away. These travel-worn strangers dressed in coarse and ragged Mongol clothing looked nothing like the handsome, well-dressed Venetian merchants Niccolò and Maffeo Polo and Niccolò's son Marco.

Finally, reluctantly, they were allowed to come in. But their relatives were very doubtful. The three returned travelers planned a big surprise for their family and friends. They invited the most important families in Venice to a big feast. Of course everyone talked of nothing else for days before.

According to one story that was told about their return, Maffeo's wife gave his old ragged traveling clothes to a beggar while her husband was preparing for the banquet. She didn't know that he and his brother and nephew had sewn their entire fortune—the precious jewels that Kublai Khan had given them—into the seams of their clothing. It was the practice of travelers to dress like poor men so robbers wouldn't be tempted to steal from them. Maffeo was enraged. Clever as he was, he soon thought of a way to get his clothes back.

He went to one of the busiest bridges in Venice and set up a strange spinning wheel. There was no yarn to be spun, but he sat there all day spinning the wheel and muttering in an odd foreign language. Everyone in Venice crowded around to see the madman from the east. Maffeo watched the crowd carefully. Sure enough, before long he saw a beggar wearing his clothes. He took the rags back, gladly paying for them.

On the night of the big celebration, the most important people of Venice arrived at the Polo mansion. An enormous feast had been prepared, and the three travelers changed their clothing for every course that was served. First they wore magnificent suits of red satin. Then they changed to even more costly clothes of red brocade. Finally, they appeared in richly decorated red velvet.

After each change they cut up the expensive clothing and gave the pieces of fabric to their guests. This was a custom in the Mongol court. It showed how wealthy and powerful the hosts were. The Venetians were astonished at this. But they were even more astonished when, at the end of the meal, Niccolò, Maffeo, and Marco brought out their old ragged Mongol clothes and placed them on the table. Then they took sharp knives and cut open the seams. Piles of brilliant jewels tumbled out. The guests could hardly believe what they were seeing.

Of course, when it was clear that the returned merchants were very wealthy, family and friends accepted them gladly. They resumed their life as Venetian businessmen, buying and selling and increasing the family fortune. To further their trading business, Marco Polo became the captain of a merchant ship that sailed to Mediterranean ports.

At this time the commercial rivalry between Genoa and Venice had become open war. All of the merchant ships were armed. Many minor sea battles and a few major ones were fought between Venetian and Genoese ships. In one of these—historians differ as to the date, but it most likely was in 1296—the Genoese captured Marco's vessel. He was taken to Genoa and placed in a building used for prisoners of the upper classes, who were treated relatively well. Even so, the prison was crowded and uncomfortable, and worst of all—for one as used to an active life of adventure as Marco—boring.

One of Marco's fellow prisoners was from Pisa. His name was Rustichello, and he was a writer of medieval romances. He was particularly known for his stories of King Arthur and the Knights of the Round Table. The two prisoners began talking, since there was little else to do. When he heard the stories that Marco told about his travels, Rustichello realized that here was the real thing: a fantastic story of adventure that had actually happened. He proposed that he and Marco should collaborate on a book.

Marco agreed and sent a message to Venice, asking his father to send him all the notebooks he had compiled during his journeys. Surprisingly, the jailers allowed Marco Polo's notes to be delivered. Possibly the guards had also listened to his wonderful stories and wanted to hear more. Marco and Rustichello set to work. The book was finished in the spring of 1299. At about the same time the war between Genoa and Venice ended. Marco was released from prison. He returned to Venice.

What we now know as *The Travels of Marco Polo* was published soon afterward as *A Description of the World*. It was written in French, the usual language in which medieval romances were written and the one Rustichello had used for his other books. Very soon it was translated into Latin. It became popular all over Europe and appeared in Spanish, German, and English, as well as some Italian dialects. No other book of this era was as widely translated during its author's lifetime. But although people enjoyed the book, they read it as a tale of fantasy and adventure, like other medieval romances. They didn't realize that it was an actual account of a real man's travels and observations.

Marco Polo continued his business as a merchant and was very successful. He married a young woman named Donata Badoer shortly after he returned from prison. They had three daughters, Fantina, Bellela, and Moreta. Marco's father, Niccolò, died around 1300. Marco and his uncle Maffeo continued the family business together until Maffeo's death some 10 or 15 years later. Maffeo had no children and left all his property to his nephew.

As Marco grew older his memory returned more and more often to his experiences in Asia. His family and friends may have grown tired of his stories, which they had never really believed. They called him Il Milione (the million) because they said he told a million lies.

Marco Polo lived to be 69. He became seriously ill in December of 1323, and by early January the following year it was obvious that he was dying. A priest was called. A notary wrote down the provisions of the dying man's will. He left his property to his wife and children, freed the Tartar servant who had remained with him all those years, and gave money to various people and organizations.

According to legend, just before Marco Polo died on January 8, the priest told him not to die in sin. He asked Marco if he finally wanted to confess that the stories he had told were lies. Instead of a confession, the great explorer said, "I did not tell half of what I saw, for I knew I would not be believed."[1]

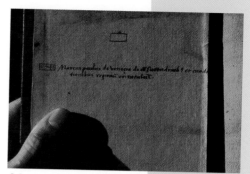

Marco Polo titled his book about his travels A Description of the World. *This is the edition of Marco Polo's book that Christopher Columbus took with him on his own journeys of exploration.*

Only gradually over the next three or four hundred years did the world come to understand that Marco Polo had written an accurate account of his travels in Asia. Other explorers and travelers, one by one, were able to confirm that many of Marco's reports were accurate.

Yet even today, there is skepticism about how much of what Marco wrote can actually be believed. For example, he never mentions the Great Wall of China, which to some people raises doubts as to whether he was ever in China. Some of the descriptions are taken almost word for word from Rustichello's own books. On the other hand, the book includes many details that only a person who actually saw them could have written. And many explorers, such as Christopher Columbus, carried a copy of the book with them.

There can be little doubt that Marco "produced one of the most influential books of the Middle Ages," as John Lanford observes. "It is no exaggeration to say that never before or since has one man given such an immense body of new geographical knowledge."[2]

FYI
For Your Info

After a lengthy period of decline, the Roman Empire finally fell in the late 400s. That gave rise to the Middle Ages, an era of about 1,000 years that is also known as the medieval period. It lasted until about 1500 when the Renaissance (which means "rebirth") began.

Instead of stable national governments, there were hundreds of feudal states. These were areas governed by a nobleman with enough soldiers to protect his territory. As the Roman Empire broke up into these little feudal states, its language, Latin, broke up into different dialects. These dialects eventually became such modern languages as French, Spanish, and Italian. In fact, the word "romance" comes from the Old French word "romanz," which meant "the speech of the people."

This era is sometimes referred to as "the dark ages." What was dark about it? Constant warfare, for one thing. The period was also "dark" because most people were ignorant. Very few could read Latin, the language of learning. A third reason for "darkness" was the difficult living conditions. Poverty was widespread and people spent most of their time working. Having little other entertainment, they enjoyed stories of adventure. Many of these stories were long narratives called medieval romances.

The writers of medieval romances would use what they knew of history or of classical literature. Heroes such as Alexander the Great or King Arthur and his Knights of the Round Table would go on fantastic journeys, doing battle with dragons and other supernatural creatures. The heroes were always brave, virtuous, and loyal to their feudal lord. A love element frequently entered into these stories, as the heroes would protect princesses and rescue them from danger.

The more fantastic and unrealistic the medieval romances were, the better people liked them. The stories provided an escape from the drudgery of everyday life. Even though the writers used as many devices of magic and fantasy as they could, they presented the stories as though they were factual reports of the real adventures of historical heroes.

Chronology

1253	Father Niccolò and uncle Maffeo leave Venice for Constantinople
1254	Marco Polo is born in Venice
1260	Niccolò and Maffeo leave Constantinople and travel to the east
1265	Ambassadors convince the Polo brothers to travel to the court of Kublai Khan
1269	Sees father for the first time as the Polo brothers return to Venice
1271	Leaves Venice with his father and uncle to travel to China
1272	Arrives at Persian Gulf
1275	Arrives at the summer palace of Kublai Khan
1280	Begins expeditions to the southern provinces of Kublai Khan's empire
1288	Goes by sea to India; Persian ambassadors seek royal princess to be new wife of Persian Khan
1292	Sails from China to escort royal princess to Persia
1295	Returns to Venice
1296	Captured in a sea battle with Genoese ships and taken to prison in Genoa; while in prison he and another prisoner, Rustichello, write the book about his travels
1299	Released from prison when war between Venice and Genoa ends; publishes *A Description of the World*; marries Donata Badoer
1300	Father dies
1324	Dies in Venice on January 8

BIOGRAPHY FROM
ANCIENT CIVILIZATIONS
LEGENDS, FOLKLORE, AND STORIES OF ANCIENT WORLDS

Timeline in History

1187	Pope Gregory VIII proclaims the Third Crusade to fight Islamic leader Saladin.
1202	Pope Innocent III initiates the Fourth Crusade to recover holy places; instead the Crusaders attack Constantinople.
1206	United Mongol tribes declare Genghis Kahn their supreme ruler.
1209	Saint Francis of Assisi founds the Franciscan order.
1212	The Children's Crusade begins; thousands of European children die of starvation and exposure or are sold into slavery.
1215	English barons force King John to sign the Magna Carta.
1221	The Chinese use gunpowder in bombs for the first time.
1227	Saint Thomas Aquinas is born in Naples; Genghis Khan dies; Gregory IX is elected Pope.
1228	Emperor Frederick II leads the Sixth Crusade and is crowned King of Jerusalem in 1229.
1231	King Henry VIII patronizes England's Cambridge University.
1258	Mongol chief Hulagu Khan captures the city of Baghdad.
1272	Mongol warriors begin the conquest of Burma.
1279	China's Song dynasty falls to Kublai Khan; Mongols control all of China.
1281	Mongol warriors attempt to invade Japan but are swept away by a typhoon which the Japanese call *kamikaze*, or "divine wind."
1288	The first known gun, a small cannon, is constructed in China.
1307	Italian poet Dante Alighieri begins to write the *Divine Comedy*.
1321	Dante dies.
1336	Tamerlane, the last great nomadic leader, is born.
1338	The Hundred Years War between England and France begins.
1346	The Black Plague begins; it kills between 20 percent and 40 percent of the population of Europe in the next seven years.
1354	An elaborate mechanical clock with angels, hourglasses, and crowing roosters is constructed and installed in Strasbourg Cathedral.
1368	The Mongols are defeated and ousted from China; Chinese Ming Dynasty is founded.
1370	*Gawain and the Green Knight* is written in England.
1387	English poet Geoffrey Chaucer begins writing *The Canterbury Tales*.

Chapter Notes

CHAPTER ONE   **THE RETURN**

1. Marco Polo, *The Travels of Marco Polo*, trans. Ronald Latham (New York: Penguin Books, 1982), p. 37.

The dialogue in this chapter represents the author's interpretation of what might have happened, based on her extensive research, and is solely an aid to readability.

CHAPTER TWO   **THE ADVENTURE BEGINS**

1. John Larner, *Marco Polo and the Discovery of the World* (New Haven, CT: Yale University Press, 1999), p. 37.

2. Henry H. Hart, *Venetian Adventurer: Being an Account of the Life and Times and of the Book of Messer Marco Polo* (Stanford, CA: Stanford University Press, 1942), p. 49.

3. Ibid.

4. Ibid., p. 60.

5. Marco Polo, *The Travels of Marco Polo, trans. Ronald Latham* (New York: Penguin Books, 1982), p. 37.

6. R. P. Lister, *Marco Polo's Travels in Xanadu with Kublai Khan* (London: Gordon Cremonesi Ltd., 1976), p. 36.

7. Polo, p. 48.

8. Ibid., pp. 66–67.

CHAPTER THREE   **KUBLAI KHAN**

1. Marco Polo, *The Travels of Marco Polo, trans. Ronald Latham* (New York: Penguin Books, 1982), p. 40.

2. Ibid., p. 151.

3. Ibid., pp. 121–22.

CHAPTER FOUR   **THE JOURNEYS**

1. Marco Polo, *The Travels of Marco Polo*, trans. Ronald Latham (New York: Penguin Books, 1982), p. 97.

2. Ibid, p. 101.

3. Ibid.

4. Leonardo Olschki, *Marco Polo's Asia* (Berkeley: University of California Press, 1960), p. 181.

5. Polo, p. 45.

6. Henry H. Hart, *Venetian Adventurer: Being an Account of the Life and Times and of the Book of Messer Marco Polo* (Stanford, CA: Stanford University Press, 1942), p. 168.

CHAPTER FIVE   **PRISON**

1. Richard Humble, *Marco Polo* (New York: G. P. Putnam's Sons, 1975), p. 209.

2. John Larner, *Marco Polo and the Discovery of the World* (New Haven, CT: Yale University Press, 1999), p. 1.

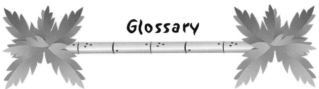

Glossary

ambassador	(am-BASS-uh-dur) a high-ranking official who represents his government in a foreign nation.
brocade	(broh-KAYD) a rich fabric with raised patterns woven in gold or silver thread.
canal	(cuh-NAL) artificial waterway used for navigation.
cargo	(KAR-goh) the goods or products carried by a ship.
courier	(KOO-ree-ur) a special messenger.
crusade	(krew-SAYD) a war undertaken for religious reasons.
dialect	(DYE-uh-lekt) a regional form of a language differing from the standard form.
drought	(DROUT) a long period of dry weather.
execution	(ex-uh-KEW-shun) inflicting the death penalty.
feudal state	(FEW-dul STAYT) a province controlled by one nobleman.
fluent	(FLEW-unt) showing ease and command in speaking another language.
friar	(FRY-uhr) a member of a religious order.
khan	(KON) the title of Mongol emperors during the Middle Ages.
looting	(LEW-ting) stealing things, particularly during a war or period of civil disorder.
medieval	(mee-dee-EEV-ul) relating to the Middle Ages, from about 500 to 1500.
merchandise	(MUR-chun-dice) goods bought and sold.
mosaic	(moh-ZAY-ik) decorations or pictures made from small pieces of glass or stone.
nomadic	(no-MAD-ik) wandering from place to place in search of pasture for animals.
plunder	(PLUN-dur) to take things by force, particularly during war.
Pope	(POHP) the head of the Roman Catholic Church.
quay	(KEY) a dock for loading and unloading ships.

For Further Reading

For Young Adults

Ceserani, Gian Paolo. *Marco Polo*. New York: G. P. Putnam's Sons, 1977.

Humble, Richard. *The Travels of Marco Polo*. New York: Franklin Watts, 1990.

Kent, Zachary. *The World's Great Explorers: Marco Polo*. Chicago: Children's Press, 1992.

Marcovitz, Hal. *Marco Polo and the Wonders of the East*. Philadelphia: Chelsea House Publishers, 2000.

Walsh, Richard J. *The Adventures and Discoveries of Marco Polo*. New York: Random House, 1953.

Works Consulted

Hart, Henry H. *Venetian Adventurer: Being an Account of the Life and Times and of the Book of Messer Marco Polo*. Stanford, CA: Stanford University Press, 1942.

Humble, Richard. *Marco Polo*. New York: G. P. Putnam's Sons, 1975.

Larner, John. *Marco Polo and the Discovery of the World*. New Haven, CT: Yale University Press, 1999.

Lister, R. P. *Marco Polo's Travels in Xanadu with Kublai Khan*. London: Gordon Cremonesi Ltd., 1976.

Olschki, Leonardo. *Marco Polo's Asia*. Berkeley: University of California Press, 1960.

Polo, Marco. *The Travels of Marco Polo*. Translated by Ronald Latham. New York: Penguin Books, 1982.

On the Internet

Marco Polo and His Travels
http://www.silk-road.com/art1/marcopolo.shtml

Marco Polo's Asia
http://www.tk421.net/essays/polo.html

The Travels of Marco Polo
http://website.lineone.net/~mcrouch/marcopolo/marcopolo.htm

Marco Polo, Catholic Encyclopedia
http://www.newadvent.org/cathen/12217a.htm

Marco Polo Homepage: biography and images
http://www.susqu.edu/history/medtrav/MarcoPolo/

History of Silk
http://www.silk-road.com/artl/silkhistory.shtml

Crusades
http://www.worldhistory.com/crusades.htm

Index